ATTACK OF THE
Deranged Mutant
Killer Monster
SNOW GOONS

Also by Bill Watterson:

CALVIN AND HOBBES
SOMETHING UNDER THE BED IS DROOLING
YUKON HO!
WEIRDOS FROM ANOTHER PLANET
THE REVENGE OF THE BABY-SAT
THE CALVIN AND HOBBES LAZY SUNDAY BOOK
THE AUTHORITATIVE CALVIN AND HOBBES
SCIENTIFIC PROGRESS GOES 'BOINK'
THE INDISPENSABLE CALVIN AND HOBBES
THE DAYS ARE JUST PACKED
HOMICIDAL PSYCHO JUNGLE CAT
ESSENTIAL CALVIN AND HOBBES
CALVIN AND HOBBES: THE TENTH ANNIVERSARY
THERE'S TREASURE EVERYWHERE
IT'S A MAGICAL WORLD

ATTACK OF THE Deranged Mutant Killer Monster SNOW GOONS

A Calvin and Hobbes Collection by Bill Watterson

sphere

SPHERE

First published in the USA by Andrews McMeel Publishing 1992
First published in Great Britain in 1992
by Warner Books
Reprinted 1992, 1993, 1994, 1995, 1996, 1997, 1999, 2001
Reprinted by Time Warner Paperbacks in 2002
Reprinted 2003
Reprinted by Time Warner Books in 2006
Reprinted by Sphere in 2007, 2009
Reprinted by Sphere in 2001, 2009, 2011, 2012, 2017, 2019, 2021
Copyright © 1992 by Bill Watterson, distributed by
Universal Press Syndicate

ISBN: 978-0-7515-0933-5

Printed and bound in Malta by
Gutenberg Press Limited

Sphere
An imprint of
Little, Brown Book Group
Carmelite House
50 Victoria Embankment
London EC4Y 0DZ

An Hachette UK Company
www.hachette.co.uk

www.littlebrown.co.uk

CALVIN and HOBBES

by WATTERSON

I'D SURE LIKE TO SHAKE THE HAND OF THE GENIUS WHO INVENTED THESE.

OK, HERE'S THE GAME: WE TOSS THE WATER BALLOON BACK AND FORTH, BUT EACH TIME WE CATCH IT, WE TAKE A STEP BACK. THE IDEA IS TO SEE HOW FAR APART WE CAN GET BEFORE ONE OF US GETS SOAKED.

GOTCHA.

OK, TOSS IT TO ME.

THERE, I CAUGHT IT! NOW WE TAKE A STEP BACK, AND I'LL TOSS IT TO *YOU*.

HA HA! CATCH *THIS*, SUCKER!

PLOOSH!

HA HA HA! WHAT A CHUMP! WHAT A NAÏF! HA HA HA!

HEY! WHAT'S THE MATTER? CAN'T YOU TAKE A JOKE?! IT WAS A *JOKE*! I MEAN, IT WAS AN *ACCIDENT*! I DIDN'T DO IT ON PURPOSE!

HEY! NO! NOT THE RAIN BARREL!

IT'S NO FUN TO PLAY GAMES WITH A POOR SPORT.

CAN I BE EXCUSED? THERE'S A TV SHOW I WANT TO SEE.

WE'RE STILL EATING DINNER, CALVIN.

I'M THROUGH. THIS STUFF WAS AWFUL. I WANT TO GO WATCH TELEVISION.

IT'S IMPOLITE TO LEAVE THE TABLE IN THE MIDDLE OF A MEAL.

SO WHAT AM I SUPPOSED TO DO? JUST SIT HERE AND WATCH YOU GUYS CHEW?! I'LL MISS MY SHOW!

YOUR TV SHOW ISN'T AS IMPORTANT AS SPENDING SOME TIME TOGETHER AS A FAMILY.

WE'LL COMPROMISE. I'LL GO WATCH A SITCOM FAMILY.

IN A MINUTE YOU'RE GOING TO DISCOVER THE DIFFERENCE BETWEEN THOSE AND REAL LIFE.

MY TV SHOW IS STARTING. I'M MISSING MY SHOW!

I'M SURE YOUR INSTINCT FOR SURVIVAL WILL KICK IN SHORTLY.

WHAT'S THE BIG DEAL ABOUT DINNER?! WHY CAN'T I GO WATCH TV? LOTS OF PEOPLE WATCH TV WHILE THEY EAT!

CALVIN, DINNER IS THE ONE TIME DURING THE DAY THAT WE SET ASIDE TO BE TOGETHER AND TALK. THERE'S MORE TO BEING A FAMILY THAN JUST LIVING IN THE SAME HOUSE. WE NEED TO INTERACT ONCE IN A WHILE.

WE COULD ALL ARGUE OVER WHAT CHANNEL TO WATCH.

YOU KNOW WHAT I MEAN.

I'VE MISSED HALF OF MY TV SHOW NOW. I HOPE YOU'RE HAPPY.

YOU SHOULDN'T BE PLANNING YOUR LIFE AROUND THE TV ANYWAY.

HMPH.

LOOK, I DON'T THINK IT'S TOO MUCH TO ASK THAT WE SIT TOGETHER FOR 40 MINUTES WITHOUT DISTRACTIONS AND INTERRUPTIONS.

RINNGG!

I'LL GET IT! I'M EXPECTING A CALL.

GO AHEAD, DAD. I BELIEVE YOU WERE SAYING SOMETHING FUNNY.

I HAVE ALL THESE GREAT GENES, BUT THEY'RE RECESSIVE. THAT'S THE PROBLEM HERE.

C'MON HOBBES, WE HAVE TO GO OUTSIDE.

WE *HAVE* TO?

YEAH, DAD WON'T LET ME WATCH TV. HE SAYS IT'S SUMMER, IT'S LIGHT LATE, AND I SHOULD GO RUN AROUND INSTEAD OF SITTING IN FRONT OF THE TUBE. CAN YOU BELIEVE IT?! WHAT A DICTATOR!

HOW CRUEL IT IS TO BE FORCED TO PLAY.

I'LL SHOW HIM. I REFUSE TO HAVE FUN.

OK, NEXT WE'LL RACE TO THAT TREE OVER THERE.

THIS RACE WILL DETERMINE THE CHAMPIONSHIP OF THE UNIVERSE.

OH... WAIT. HOW LONG HAVE WE BEEN OUT HERE?

I DUNNO. AN HOUR MAYBE.

REALLY? GEEZ, WHERE DOES THE TIME GO?! HANG ON, I'LL BE RIGHT BACK.

I'M *NOT* HAVING FUN!

IT'S GETTING DARK, CALVIN. TIME TO COME IN AND GO TO BED!

BUT HOBBES AND I WERE CATCHING FIREFLIES. CAN'T WE STAY OUT A LITTLE LONGER?

HA! FIRST YOU DIDN'T WANT TO GO OUT, AND NOW YOU DON'T WANT TO COME IN!

SEE, BY NOT WATCHING TV, YOU HAD MORE FUN, AND NOW YOU'LL HAVE MEMORIES OF SOMETHING REAL YOU *DID*, INSTEAD OF SOMETHING FAKE YOU JUST *WATCHED*.

NOTHING SPOILS FUN LIKE FINDING OUT IT BUILDS CHARACTER.

CALVIN and HOBBES by WATTERSON

THE LATE CRETACEOUS...

..WHEN THE WORLD MEANT BUSINESS!

A GIGANTIC QUETZALCOATLUS, A PTEROSAUR THE SIZE OF AN AIRPLANE, SWOOPS OVER THE HORRIBLE TYRANNOSAURUS!

THE TYRANNOSAUR LUNGES AND BRINGS DOWN THE FLYING PEST!

UH OH! THE COMMOTION ATTRACTS OTHER TYRANNOSAURS, GREEDY FOR AN UNDESERVED PIECE!

PLEASE PASS ME A WING, CALVIN.

NO! YOU CAN'T HAVE ANY! IT'S MINE! ALL MINE!

DRIVEN AWAY BY THE FIERCE ROARING AND GNASHING OF THE INTRUDERS, THE TYRANNOSAUR NURSES A DEEP GRUDGE. REVENGE WILL SOON BE HIS!

10

11

CALVIN, WILL YOU TAKE THIS TO THE GARBAGE CAN IN THE GARAGE PLEASE?

THE *GARAGE*?? ARE YOU MAD?

I *WILL* BE, IF YOU DON'T HOP TO IT.

BUT THAT'S WHERE MY KILLER BICYCLE IS! I CAN'T GO OUT THERE! IT'LL JUMP ME!

I DON'T WANT ANY NONSENSE. JUST DO WHAT I ASKED, OK?

RRRRR

I WONDER HOW FAR FROM THIS HOUSE MY SAVINGS WOULD GET ME.

PSST! HOBBES!

WHAT ARE YOU DOING UP THERE?

HIDING FROM MY KILLER BICYCLE. IT CAN'T CLIMB TREES, SO I GUESS I'LL STAY HERE THE REST OF MY LIFE.

YOU SHOULD JUST WEDGE A BIG STICK THROUGH THE SPOKES OF THE FRONT WHEEL. THAT WAY WHEN THE STICK HITS THE FORK, THE WHEEL WILL JAM AND THE BIKE WILL FLIP OVER.

HEY, THAT'S A *GREAT* IDEA! HOBBES, YOU'RE A LIFESAVER!

WE COULD MOSEY OVER TO THE KITCHEN IF YOU'RE WONDERING HOW YOU CAN POSSIBLY THANK ME ENOUGH.

I DID IT, HOBBES! I DID JUST WHAT YOU SAID! I PUT A STICK IN THE SPOKES OF MY KILLER BICYCLE!

WHEN IT TRIED TO CHASE ME, IT FLIPPED OVER! I WRESTLED IT TO EXHAUSTION, AND THEN I LET THE AIR OUT OF ITS TIRES!

HA! I GUESS THAT NASTY OL' THING WON'T BE COMING AFTER *ME* ANY MORE! WE'RE TOO SMART FOR IT! MAN TRIUMPHS OVER MACHINE!

TRAINING WHEELS! WHAT A GOOD IDEA!

I PUMPED UP HIS TIRES TOO. THEY WERE BOTH FLAT.

Calvin and Hobbes

by WATTERSON

BOOGER BALLS ARE ILLEGAL!

WHAP!

FIRST BASE!

FIFTH!

NINTH!

PUFF PUFF
ELEVENTH!
PUFF

TWENTY-FIFTH! CALVIN'S GOING FOR HOME!

TOO LATE! YOU'RE OUT!

DOINK

I THINK WE NEED TO CHANGE THE RULES

OH, YOU WANT TO PLAY THE SISSY WAY NOW, I BET.

15

MY TIGER, IT SEEMS, IS RUNNING 'ROUND NUDE.
THIS FUR COAT MUST HAVE MADE HIM PERSPIRE.
IT LIES ON THE FLOOR– SHOULD THIS BE CONSTRUED
AS A PERMANENT CHANGE OF ATTIRE?
PERHAPS HE CONSIDERS ITS COLORS PASSÉ,
OR MAYBE IT FIT HIM TOO SNUG
WILL HE WANT IT BACK? SHOULD I PUT IT AWAY?
OR USE IT RIGHT HERE AS A RUG?

Calvin and Hobbes

by WATTERSON

ANOTHER DAY, ANOTHER DOLLAR...

... ANOTHER IRREPLACEABLE CHUNK OUT OF A FINITE AND RAPIDLY PASSING LIFETIME.

WHAT A BEAUTIFUL SUMMER DAY... AND I'VE GOT TO SPEND IT IN AN OFFICE. BROTHER.

IT SEEMS LIKE I'M ALWAYS RUSHING OFF AND NEVER TAKING THE TIME TO ENJOY DAYS LIKE THIS.

I'D SURE LIKE TO HAVE A QUIET DAY AROUND THE HOUSE. NO TRAFFIC, NO SCHEDULE, NO PHONE CALLS... BOY, THAT WOULD BE GREAT. I COULD SPEND SOME TIME WITH CALVIN, READ A BOOK, GO ON A BIKE RIDE...

MAYBE I SHOULD TAKE THE DAY OFF. THE WORLD WOULDN'T END IF I DIDN'T GO INTO THE OFFICE TODAY. DAYS LIKE THIS DON'T COME OFTEN AND LIFE IS SHORT.

WATTERSON

HI DAD. BYE DAD.

NUGHH

YOU GET BACK HERE AND PICK EVERY ONE OF THOSE DEAD BUGS OUT OF MY SHAMPOO.!! I MEAN NOW!

WITH A DISTANT RUMBLING, GREAT THUNDER CLOUDS PILE HIGH INTO THE SKY!

SUDDENLY THERE'S A BLINDING FLASH OF LIGHT! IT'S CALVIN THE LIGHTNING BOLT!

IN A FRACTION OF A SECOND, THE HOUSE BELOW WILL BE IN A MILLION PIECES!

I KNOW IT'S RAINING OUT, BUT PLAY A BOARD GAME OR SOMETHING.

EVERY DAY IT'S THE SAME OLD THING.

... BUT NOT TODAY!

EVERYBODY'S A SLAVE TO ROUTINE.

CAN I GET SOME CONTACT LENSES?

YOUR EYES ARE FINE! YOU DON'T NEED CONTACTS.

YES I DO! THEY HAVE SOME THAT CHANGE THE COLOR OF YOUR EYES!

YOUR EYES ARE VERY PRETTY THE WAY THEY ARE.

BUT IF I HAD CONTACTS, I COULD MAKE ONE EYE BLOOD RED AND THE OTHER YELLOW STRIPED, LIKE A BUG.

I DUNNO, IT SEEMS LIKE ONCE PEOPLE GROW UP, THEY HAVE NO IDEA WHAT'S COOL.

20

CaLViN and HObbEs

by WATTERSON

TO MAKE INSTANT FUN...

... JUST ADD WATER!

SQUEAK

HEH HEH HEH   FWOOSH

HEE HEE

LOOKING FOR SOMEONE?

UH, WHO? *NE??* HA HA HA HA HA! UM, NO-O. I MEAN, YES...BUT SOMEONE *ELSE*. HEH HEH. NOT YOU.

HERE'S A HYPOTHETICAL QUESTION YOU SHOULD ASK YOURSELF.

IF YOU KNEW TODAY WAS YOUR LAST DAY ON EARTH, WHAT WOULD YOU DO DIFFERENT?

...*ESPECIALLY* IF, BY DOING SOMETHING *DIFFERENT*, TODAY MIGHT *NOT* BE YOUR LAST DAY ON EARTH.

I DON'T THINK THAT QUESTION WAS VERY HYPOTHETICAL AT ALL.

WATTERSON

21

CALVIN AND HOBBES

by WATTERSON

HOW LONG TILL YOU'RE DONE?

AT LEAST 15 MINUTES, PLUS DRYING.

...SIGHHHH...

I'M BORED. THERE'S NOTHING TO DO.

NOTHING TO DO ?!? IT'S A BEAUTIFUL SUMMER DAY!

YOU'VE GOT THE WHOLE OUTDOORS TO PLAY IN! IF YOU CAN'T FIND SOMETHING TO DO, IT'S BECAUSE YOU HAVEN'T TRIED. GO ON! USE SOME IMAGINATION!

MY UPBRINGING IS FILLED WITH INCONSISTENT MESSAGES.

CalViN and HObbEs

by WATTERSON

SHEESH. YOU BUY THE KID A GOOD, EXPENSIVE LOCK, AND LOOK.

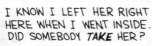

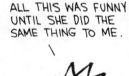

HELP ME WITH THIS HOMEWORK, OK? WHAT'S 6+3?

6+3, EH? WELL, THIS ONE IS A BIT TRICKY.

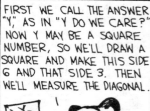

FIRST WE CALL THE ANSWER "Y," AS IN "Y DO WE CARE?" NOW Y MAY BE A SQUARE NUMBER, SO WE'LL DRAW A SQUARE AND MAKE THIS SIDE 6 AND THAT SIDE 3. THEN WE'LL MEASURE THE DIAGONAL.

I DON'T REMEMBER THE TEACHER EXPLAINING IT LIKE THIS.

SHE PROBABLY DOESN'T KNOW HIGHER MATH. WHEN YOU DEAL WITH HIGH NUMBERS, YOU NEED HIGHER MATH.

BUT THIS DIAGONAL IS JUST A LITTLE UNDER TWO.

OK, HERE, I'LL DRAW A BIGGER SQUARE.

HEY, NO COMIC BOOKS UNTIL YOU FINISH YOUR HOMEWORK.

I DID FINISH.

THAT DIDN'T TAKE VERY LONG. DID YOU DO A GOOD JOB?

I DID A GREAT JOB. WHEN YOU'RE AS FAR AHEAD OF THE CLASS AS I AM, IT DOESN'T TAKE MUCH TIME.

WELL WE'LL SEE ABOUT THAT WHEN I GET BACK FROM MY PARENT-TEACHER CONFERENCE WITH MISS WORMWOOD.

YOU'RE GOING TO TALK TO MY TEACHER?

I'M SURE IT WILL BE AN INFORMATIVE MEETING.

GOSH, I FORGOT TO TELL YOU! MISS WORMWOOD SAID I WAS SO GOOD, YOU DIDN'T NEED TO BOTHER COMING! REALLY! SHE SAID YOU DON'T HAVE TO GO!

OH MAN! MOM WENT TO A PARENT-TEACHER CONFERENCE! I'M AS GOOD AS DEAD! MISS WORMWOOD WILL TELL MOM ALL SORTS OF HORROR STORIES ABOUT ME!

HORROR STORIES?

WELL, IT'S ALL A QUESTION OF PERSPECTIVE. STILL, I THINK I SHOULD BE ALLOWED TO HAVE A LAWYER PRESENT AT THE MEETING.

WHAT ARE YOU GOING TO SAY WHEN YOUR MOM GETS BACK?

NOTHING.

NOTHING AT ALL?

BUDDY, IF YOU THINK I'M EVEN GOING TO BE HERE, YOU'RE CRAZY!

I'M HOME.

HOW WAS YOUR MEETING WITH CALVIN'S TEACHER?

WELL, WHEN WE GOT TO THE CLASSROOM, WE SAW THAT ALL THE KIDS HAD DRAWN SELF-PORTRAITS IN ART CLASS, AND HAD LEFT THE PICTURES ON THEIR DESKS SO THE PARENTS WOULD RECOGNIZE THEIR CHILD'S SEAT.

THAT'S A CUTE IDEA. DID YOU FIND CALVIN'S PICTURE?

THERE WAS ONE DRAWING OF A GREEN KID WITH FANGS, SIX EYES, AND HIS FINGER UP HIS NOSE.

UH OH.

THE MEETING WENT DOWNHILL FROM THERE.

CALVIN, I...

YIKE!! YOU'RE HOME! I DIDN'T EVEN FINISH PACK... ..THAT IS, UM...

LIES! EVERYTHING MISS WORMWOOD SAID ABOUT ME WAS A LIE! SHE JUST DOESN'T LIKE ME! SHE HATES LITTLE BOYS! IT'S NOT *MY* FAULT! *I'M* NOT TO BLAME!

SHE TOLD YOU ABOUT THE NOODLES, RIGHT? IT WASN'T ME! NOBODY SAW ME! I WAS FRAMED! I WOULDN'T DO ANYTHING LIKE THAT! I'M INNOCENT, I TELL YOU!

WHAT NOODLES?

OH .... UH.... HA HA! DID I SAY NOODLES? YOU MUST HAVE HEARD WRONG. I DIDN'T SAY NOODLES.

OK CALVIN, LET'S CHECK OVER YOUR MATH HOMEWORK.

LET'S NOT, AND SAY WE DID.

YOUR TEACHER SAYS YOU NEED TO SPEND MORE TIME ON IT. HAVE A SEAT.

MORE TIME?! I ALREADY SPENT TEN WHOLE MINUTES ON IT! TEN MINUTES SHOT! WASTED! DOWN THE DRAIN!

YOU'VE WRITTEN HERE 8+4=7. NOW YOU KNOW THAT'S NOT RIGHT.

SO I WAS OFF A LITTLE BIT. SUE ME.

YOU CAN'T *ADD* THINGS AND COME OUT WITH *LESS* THAN YOU STARTED WITH!

I CAN DO THAT! IT'S A FREE COUNTRY! I'VE GOT MY RIGHTS!

A SMALL RED SPACECRAFT BREAKS THROUGH THE CLOUD COVER OF MYSTERIO SYSTEM PLANET 6!

AT THE CONTROLS, IT'S NONE OTHER THAN OUR FEARLESS HERO, SPACEMAN SPIFF!

PILOTING OVER THE LIFELESS WORLD, HE REFLECTS ON HIS UNUSUAL MISSION...

QUIZ:
1. 6 + 5 = ___

...TO SOMEHOW CRASH PLANETS 6 AND 5 TOGETHER!

IN A SCIENTIFIC MISSION TO DISCOVER WHAT HAPPENS WHEN TWO PLANETS COLLIDE, SPACEMAN SPIFF DROPS ANCHOR!

THE ANCHOR CATCHES ON A HILLSIDE! SPIFF DOWNSHIFTS AND GUNS THE MOTOR!

IMPERCEPTIBLY AT FIRST, THE PLANET SLOWLY MOVES, TOWED ALONG BY OUR HERO, UNTIL...

...BREAKING ORBIT, PLANET 6 PICKS UP SPEED, HURLING TOWARD PLANET 5!

PULLED BY SPACEMAN SPIFF, PLANET 6 IS ABOUT TO COLLIDE WITH PLANET 5!

WITH NO TIME TO LOSE, OUR HERO CUTS LOOSE THE ANCHOR AND FLIES TO SAFETY!

THE PLANETS CRASH, GRINDING AND SHATTERING WITH AWFUL FORCE! PLANET 5, BEING SMALLER, IS CRUNCHED TO DUST! ONLY 6 REMAINS!

6 + 5 = 6

TIME! PASS YOUR PAPERS FORWARD.

TIME?! I JUST FINISHED THE FIRST PROBLEM!

HOW CAN OUR TIME BE UP?! I JUST DID THE FIRST PROBLEM ON THIS QUIZ! WHERE DID THE TIME GO??

GUESS! GUESS! PICK RANDOM NUMBERS! MAYBE A FEW WILL BE RIGHT BY SHEER LUCK! 15! 104! 3.! 27!

HAND IT IN, CALVIN. YOUR TIME'S UP.

SIGHHHH

DON'T FORGET WE HAVE A BET ON WHO GETS THE HIGHER GRADE.

THE BET'S OFF! I DON'T GAMBLE! NO BETS!

I GOT A PERFECT SCORE ON MY QUIZ.

YOU GOT A PERFECT SCORE??

WHAT DID YOU GET? IF YOU MISSED ANY, YOU OWE ME 25 CENTS.

I RAN OUT OF TIME! I'D HAVE HAD A PERFECT SCORE TOO IF I'D HAD A FEW MORE MINUTES!

WHAT DID YOU GET?

IT'S **BIOLOGICAL**! GIRLS MATURE FASTER THAN BOYS! YOU JUST GOT A BETTER GRADE BECAUSE YOU'RE A GIRL! IT'S NOT FAIR!

PAY UP.

MAYBE IT'S OPPOSITE DAY! MAYBE ALL THESE X's MEAN MY ANSWERS ARE **CORRECT**! MAYBE YOUR "A" IS REALLY AN "F"! THAT MUST BE IT! I WIN THE BET!

HOW DID YOU DO ON YOUR MATH QUIZ?

I FLUNKED IT ...BUT ONLY BECAUSE I RAN OUT OF TIME.

THE WORST PART, THOUGH, WAS THAT SUSIE DERKINS WON OUR BET ON WHO'D GET THE BETTER SCORE. I HAD TO PAY HER 25 CENTS.

BUT GET THIS! I CHEATED HER! I ONLY GAVE HER THREE DIMES! HA!

I THINK YOU'D BETTER STUDY HARDER.

OH, NOW DON'T YOU START ON ME.

BUTTONS.... CHECK. DIALS....... CHECK. SWITCHES... CHECK. LITTLE COLORED LIGHTS....... CHECK.

CALVIN, THE AIRLINE PILOT, IS TENTH IN LINE FOR TAKEOFF. HIS PATIENCE IS AT AN END!

IGNORING THE CONTROL TOWER'S PROTESTS, CALVIN GUNS THE ENGINES AND PASSES THE OTHER PLANES, CUTTING ACROSS LESS CROWDED RUNWAYS!

ROUNDING A CORNER, HE OPENS THE THROTTLE! STEWARDESSES EXPLAINING THE AIRCRAFT'S SAFETY FEATURES ARE HURLED TO THE REAR OF THE PLANE BY THE SUDDEN ACCELERATION!

ALL THE OTHER PLANES WATCH WITH ENVY AS CALVIN TAKES OFF AHEAD OF SCHEDULE!

BUT WHAT'S THIS?! ANOTHER PLANE HAD ALREADY RECEIVED CLEARANCE TO LAND! IT'S HEADED FOR THE SAME RUNWAY!

IT LOOKS LIKE A MID-AIR COLLISION OVER A CROWDED SUPER HIGHWAY AT RUSH HOUR! OH, WHAT A PRICE TO PAY FOR HIS HURRY!

I'M BACK! THANKS FOR WAITING SO PATIENTLY.

I COULD WAIT EVEN LONGER IF YOU'D BUY ME A *THIRD* PLANE.

Calvin and Hobbes

by WATTERSON

UH OH. HERE COMES SUSIE.

TRY NOT TO BREATHE IN.

HERE, CALVIN.

WHAT'S THIS?

IT'S AN INVITATION. MR. BUN IS HOSTING A MILK AND COOKIE PARTY IN TEN MINUTES, AND YOU AND HOBBES ARE INVITED.

WE DECLINE!

WE WOULDN'T ATTEND IF YOU PAID US! WE'VE GOT BETTER THINGS TO DO THAN SIT AROUND WITH GIRLS AND DUMB TOY ANIMALS!

FINE! DON'T COME! WHO CARES?!

WHAT A JERK. ...I WENT TO ALL THIS TROUBLE, TOO.

DON'T BE DISAPPOINTED, MR. BUN. WE CAN HAVE A NICE PARTY ALL BY OURSELVES.

PHOOEY.

HA! WE SHOWED HER! ALL GIRLS SHOULD BE SHIPPED TO PLUTO—THAT'S WHAT I SAY.

I WONDER WHAT KIND OF COOKIES THEY WERE.

YOU CAME!

WE DON'T ATTEND PARTIES. WE JUST CRASH 'EM!

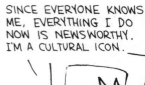

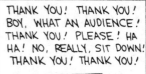

CALVIN and HOBBES by WATTERSON

OUT IN THE FARTHEST REACHES OF THE GALAXY...

...SPEEDS THAT SPLENDID SPECIMEN OF SPIRIT AND SPUNK, THE SPECTACULAR *SPACEMAN SPIFF!*

THE FEARLESS SPACEMAN SPIFF SETS OFF TO EXPLORE A NEW PLANET!

THE PLANET APPEARS TO BE UNINHABITED. THE ONLY SIGN OF LIFE IS A STRANGE LICHEN GROWING ON THE ROCKS.

NOTICING THE GEOMETRIC PATTERNS THE LICHEN FORMS, SPIFF BENDS DOWN FOR A CLOSER LOOK.

IT'S NOT LICHEN! IT'S TINY TREES ON TINY FARMLAND!

PEERING AHEAD, OUR HERO SEES A SPRAWLING CITY, WITH SKYSCRAPERS AN INCH HIGH! THE PLANET IS INHABITED AFTER ALL!

SPIFF REFLECTS THAT HUMAN SCALE IS BY NO MEANS THE STANDARD FOR LIFE FORMS.

AS IF TO DRIVE THE POINT HOME, A BLIMP-SIZED MONSTER APPEARS OVER THE HILLSIDE!

Hey, lookit Shorty here! He's playing with his fellow bugs! Haw haw!

IT'S A *Doofus Ignoramus!* OUR HERO SLOWLY REACHES FOR HIS STUN BLASTER!

WELL, IF IT ISN'T OL' ROCKET-BUTT! I GUESS YOU WON'T BE POUNCING ON *ME* ANY MORE! SEE, I'M WEARING A MASK ON THE BACK OF MY HEAD!

NOW YOU CAN'T TELL WHICH WAY I'M FACING, SO YOU CAN'T SNEAK UP FROM BEHIND! I'VE FINALLY THWARTED YOUR MURDEROUS RECREATION!

MAYBE THIS WILL TEACH YOU THAT *PEOPLE* ARE SMARTER THAN *ANIMALS!* YOU CAN'T OUTWIT A HUMAN!

NO FAIR! YOU DIDN'T EVEN SNEAK UP!

In the Middle ages, Lords and vassals lived in a Futile system.

THAT'S "FEUDAL" SYSTEM.

JUST WHEN I THOUGHT THIS JUNK WAS BEGINNING TO MAKE SENSE.

I'M A GENIUS. I CAN'T BELIEVE HOW SMART I AM.

I'VE GOT MORE BRAINS THAN I KNOW WHAT TO DO WITH.

SO I'VE NOTICED.

WOO HOO HOO

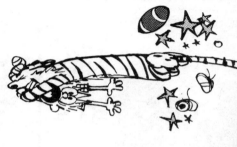

Gimme that ball or I'll punch your face in.

Smart move, sissy boy.

IN MY OPINION, WE DON'T DEVOTE NEARLY ENOUGH SCIENTIFIC RESEARCH TO FINDING A CURE FOR JERKS.

OPEN WIDE... OPEN WIDE... ...THAT'S GOOD...

NOW THIS MIGHT CAUSE SOME SLIGHT DISCOMFORT... ...HOLD REAL STILL...

RRGGHH! MMF! RRG! STOP THRASHING!.. I'VE ALMOST GOT IT..., ALMOST... MMF! *THERE!*

BOY, IT'S A GOOD THING YOU HAD THIS REMOVED! JUST LOOK AT ALL THESE BAD SPOTS!

LUNCH SHOULDN'T HAVE TO BE LIKE THIS.

TAKE A LOOK AT THIS. WOULDN'T YOU SAY THIS IS A GREAT DRAWING?

I MEAN, CAN YOU *BELIEVE* MY TEACHER DIDN'T LIKE IT?! SHE SAID IT WASN'T "SERIOUS"!

BY GOLLY, IF THIS ISN'T SERIOUS ART, THEN NOTHING IS! WHO SET MISS WORMWOOD UP AS AN ARBITER OF AESTHETICS ANYWAY? THIS IS A BEAUTIFUL WORK OF POWER AND DEPTH!

IT'S A STEGOSAURUS IN A ROCKET SHIP, RIGHT?

SEE? *YOU* UNDERSTOOD IT!

ON THE ONE HAND, IT'S A GOOD SIGN FOR US ARTISTS THAT, IN THIS AGE OF VISUAL BOMBARDMENT FROM ALL MEDIA, A SIMPLE DRAWING CAN PROVOKE AND SHOCK VIEWERS. IT CONFIRMS THAT IMAGES STILL HAVE POWER.

ON THE OTHER HAND, MY TEACHER'S REACTIONARY GRADING SHOWS THAT OUR SOCIETY IS CULTURALLY ILLITERATE AND THAT MANY PEOPLE CAN'T TELL GOOD ART FROM A HOLE IN THE GROUND.

THIS DRAWING I DID OBVIOUSLY CHALLENGES THE KNOW-NOTHING COMPLACENCY OF THOSE WHO PREFER SAFE, PREDIGESTED, BUCOLIC GENRE SCENES.

MY "C-" FIRMLY ESTABLISHES ME ON THE CUTTING EDGE OF THE AVANT-GARDE.

DON'T YOU HAVE TO WEAR SILLY CLOTHES THEN?

THE HARD PART FOR US AVANT-GARDE POST-MODERN ARTISTS IS DECIDING WHETHER OR NOT TO EMBRACE COMMERCIALISM.

DO WE ALLOW OUR WORK TO BE HYPED AND EXPLOITED BY A MARKET THAT'S SIMPLY HUNGRY FOR THE NEXT NEW THING? DO WE PARTICIPATE IN A SYSTEM THAT TURNS HIGH ART INTO LOW ART SO IT'S BETTER SUITED FOR MASS CONSUMPTION?

OF COURSE, WHEN AN ARTIST GOES COMMERCIAL, HE MAKES A MOCKERY OF HIS STATUS AS AN OUTSIDER AND FREE THINKER. HE BUYS INTO THE CRASS AND SHALLOW VALUES ART SHOULD TRANSCEND. HE TRADES THE INTEGRITY OF HIS ART FOR RICHES AND FAME.

OH, WHAT THE HECK. I'LL DO IT.

THAT WASN'T SO HARD.

TODAY I DREW ANOTHER PICTURE IN MY "DINOSAURS IN ROCKET SHIPS" SERIES, AND MISS WORMWOOD THREATENED TO GIVE ME A BAD MARK IN HER GRADE BOOK IF I DIDN'T STOP!

THE ARTS ARE UNDER ATTACK! FREEDOM OF EXPRESSION IS BEING SQUELCHED!

THE AUTHORITIES ARE TRYING TO SILENCE ANY VIEW CONTRARY TO THEIR OWN!

WHAT DOES YOUR TEACHER OBJECT TO ABOUT DINOSAURS?

MOSTLY MY DRAWING THEM DURING MATH.

CALVIN and HOBBES

by WATTERSON

CALVIN and HOBBES

by WATTERSON

Calvin and Hobbes by WATTERSON

OUT IN THE FARTHEST REACHES OF THE GALAXY...

...SPEEDS THAT SPLENDID SPECIMEN OF SPIRIT AND SPUNK, THE SPECTACULAR *SPACEMAN SPIFF!*

THE FEARLESS SPACEMAN SPIFF SETS OFF TO EXPLORE A NEW PLANET!

THE PLANET APPEARS TO BE UNINHABITED. THE ONLY SIGN OF LIFE IS A STRANGE LICHEN GROWING ON THE ROCKS.

NOTICING THE GEOMETRIC PATTERNS THE LICHEN FORMS, SPIFF BENDS DOWN FOR A CLOSER LOOK.

IT'S NOT LICHEN! IT'S TINY TREES ON TINY FARMLAND!

PEERING AHEAD, OUR HERO SEES A SPRAWLING CITY, WITH SKYSCRAPERS AN INCH HIGH! THE PLANET IS INHABITED AFTER ALL!

SPIFF REFLECTS THAT HUMAN SCALE IS BY NO MEANS THE STANDARD FOR LIFE FORMS.

AS IF TO DRIVE THE POINT HOME, A BLIMP-SIZED MONSTER APPEARS OVER THE HILLSIDE!

Hey, lookit Shorty here! He's playing with his fellow bugs! Haw haw!

IT'S A *Doofus Ignoramus!* OUR HERO SLOWLY REACHES FOR HIS STUN BLASTER!

50

VROOM
VROOOM
RRR!

VROOM
VROOOOM

AUGH!!

I WOULDN'T MIND THIS SO MUCH IF HE DIDN'T KEEP A LOG.

WOULD YOU SAY YOU WERE "VERY SURPRISED" OR "COMPLETELY SURPRISED"?

LOOK MOM, I MADE A MASK.

ARE YOU GETTING READY FOR HALLOWEEN?

HUH? NO, THIS IS FOR EVERY DAY. YOU KNOW HOW HOBBES ALWAYS SNEAKS UP FROM BEHIND AND POUNCES ON ME?

NO...

WELL, HE DOES. BUT IF YOU WEAR A MASK LIKE THIS ON THE BACK OF YOUR HEAD, TIGERS CAN'T TELL WHICH WAY YOU'RE FACING, AND THEY CAN'T SNEAK UP.

I THINK YOUR TRAIN OF THOUGHT IS A RUNAWAY.

I READ THEY WEAR THESE IN INDIA. HERE, I MADE A MASK FOR YOU TOO.

HERE, DAD. I MADE YOU A MASK LIKE MINE. YOU WEAR IT ON THE BACK OF YOUR HEAD TO PREVENT TIGER ATTACKS.

UM...

TIGERS ALWAYS TRY TO GET YOU FROM BEHIND, BUT WITH THIS MASK ON, THEY CAN'T TELL WHICH WAY YOU'RE FACING, SO THEY DON'T POUNCE. I READ IT IN A BOOK.

WELL, I APPRECIATE YOUR CONCERN, BUT I THINK I'LL TAKE MY CHANCES AND NOT LOOK LIKE A LUNATIC.

OK, IF YOU'D RATHER LOOK LIKE RAW HAMBURGER, BE MY GUEST.

HONEY, ARE WE OUT OF ASPIRIN AGAIN?

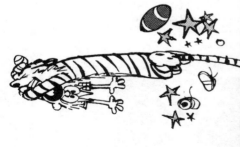

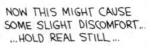

ON THE ONE HAND, IT'S A GOOD SIGN FOR US ARTISTS THAT, IN THIS AGE OF VISUAL BOMBARDMENT FROM ALL MEDIA, A SIMPLE DRAWING CAN PROVOKE AND SHOCK VIEWERS. IT CONFIRMS THAT IMAGES STILL HAVE POWER.

ON THE OTHER HAND, MY TEACHER'S REACTIONARY GRADING SHOWS THAT OUR SOCIETY IS CULTURALLY IL-LITERATE AND THAT MANY PEOPLE CAN'T TELL GOOD ART FROM A HOLE IN THE GROUND.

THIS DRAWING I DID OBVIOUSLY CHALLENGES THE KNOW-NOTHING COMPLACENCY OF THOSE WHO PREFER SAFE, PREDIGESTED, BUCOLIC GENRE SCENES.

MY "C-" FIRMLY ESTABLISHES ME ON THE CUTTING EDGE OF THE AVANT-GARDE.

DON'T YOU HAVE TO WEAR SILLY CLOTHES THEN?

THE HARD PART FOR US AVANT-GARDE POST-MODERN ARTISTS IS DECIDING WHETHER OR NOT TO EMBRACE COMMERCIALISM.

DO WE ALLOW OUR WORK TO BE HYPED AND EXPLOITED BY A MARKET THAT'S SIMPLY HUNGRY FOR THE NEXT NEW THING? DO WE PARTICIPATE IN A SYSTEM THAT TURNS HIGH ART INTO LOW ART SO IT'S BETTER SUITED FOR MASS CONSUMPTION?

OF COURSE, WHEN AN ARTIST GOES COMMERCIAL, HE MAKES A MOCKERY OF HIS STATUS AS AN OUTSIDER AND FREE THINKER. HE BUYS INTO THE CRASS AND SHALLOW VALUES ART SHOULD TRANSCEND. HE TRADES THE INTEGRITY OF HIS ART FOR RICHES AND FAME.

OH, WHAT THE HECK. I'LL DO IT.

THAT WASN'T SO HARD.

TODAY I DREW ANOTHER PICTURE IN MY "DINOSAURS IN ROCKET SHIPS" SERIES, AND MISS WORMWOOD THREATENED TO GIVE ME A BAD MARK IN HER GRADE BOOK IF I DIDN'T STOP!

THE ARTS ARE UNDER ATTACK! FREEDOM OF EXPRESSION IS BEING SQUELCHED!

THE AUTHORITIES ARE TRYING TO SILENCE ANY VIEW CONTRARY TO THEIR OWN!

WHAT DOES YOUR TEACHER OBJECT TO ABOUT DINOSAURS?

MOSTLY MY DRAWING THEM DURING MATH.

CaLviN and HobbEs

by WATTERSON

EEESH.

WHAT GOES DOWN MUST COME UP.

BLECHH!

AGKH

HEY! NO! DON'T!

UHGH

HACK COUGH SPLUTTER

MMF

BLORP!

UGHH ICKK PTOOEY

YAAA! I'LL GET YOU!

HEH HEH..

HELLO, LOCAL NAVY RECRUITMENT OFFICE? YES, THIS IS AN EMERGENCY...

60

CALVIN and HOBBES

by WATTERSON

THAT'S OUR SON! *SIGHHH*

THESE PICTURES WILL REMIND US OF MORE THAN WE WANT TO REMEMBER.

CaLViN and HobbEs

by WATTERSON

and Santa, if I gEt aNY Lords a-Leaping or GEese a-Laying, you've HAD it.

HMM... THAT MIGHT NOT BE POLITIC.

I'M GETTING NERVOUS ABOUT CHRISTMAS.

YOU'RE WORRIED YOU HAVEN'T BEEN GOOD?

THAT'S JUST THE QUESTION. IT'S ALL RELATIVE. WHAT'S SANTA'S DEFINITION? HOW GOOD DO YOU HAVE TO BE TO QUALIFY AS GOOD?

I HAVEN'T *KILLED* ANYBODY. SEE, THAT'S GOOD, RIGHT? I HAVEN'T COMMITTED ANY FELONIES. I DIDN'T START ANY WARS. I DON'T PRACTICE CANNIBALISM.

WOULDN'T YOU SAY THAT'S PRETTY GOOD? WOULDN'T YOU SAY I SHOULD GET LOTS OF PRESENTS?

BUT MAYBE GOOD IS MORE THAN THE ABSENCE OF BAD.

SEE, *THAT'S* WHAT WORRIES ME.

...OK, ASSUMING I CAN GET AN OVERNIGHT LETTER TO THE NORTH POLE, WHAT WOULD YOU CHARGE TO WRITE ME A GLOWING CHARACTER REFERENCE?

OH NO, I'M NOT GOING TO PERJURE MYSELF FOR YOU! *MY* RECORD'S CLEAN!

WELL, THE SHOPPING IS DONE, THE PRESENTS ARE WRAPPED AND SENT, AND CALVIN'S IN BED. FOR THE FIRST TIME THIS MONTH, THERE'S NOTHING THAT HAS TO BE DONE.

I KNOW... SOMETIMES THIS SEASON REALLY SEEMS OUT OF CONTROL. WE DON'T OFTEN THINK ABOUT WHAT IT'S ALL SUPPOSED TO MEAN.

MM-HMM. IT'S GOOD TO SIT BY A COZY FIRE AND TAKE SOME QUIET TIME TO REFLECT.

WHAT'S *THIS?!* SANTA FLAMBÉ?!?

PSST! WAKE UP! MERRY CHRISTMAS, OL' BUDDY!

MERRY CHRISTMAS.

I DIDN'T GET YOU A PRESENT, BUT YOU'RE MY BEST FRIEND IN THE WORLD, HOBBES.

YOU'RE MY BEST FRIEND, TOO. I THINK THAT'S A GREAT GIFT.

WELL, ENOUGH OF THAT! IT'S ALMOST 4 AM! LET'S WAKE MOM AND DAD AND SEE WHAT SANTA BROUGHT US!

REMEMBER WE AGREED THAT IF SANTA GAVE YOU ANY SALMON, YOU'D SHARE IT!

DEAR GRANDMA,

THANK YOU FOR THE NICE BOX OF CRAYONS YOU SENT ME FOR CHRISTMAS.

THIS IS PROMPT.

OH YEAH, I ALWAYS SEND GRANDMA A THANK-YOU NOTE RIGHT AWAY.

...EVER SINCE SHE SENT ME THAT EMPTY BOX WITH THE SARCASTIC NOTE SAYING SHE WAS JUST CHECKING TO SEE IF THE POSTAL SERVICE WAS STILL WORKING.

THIS WILL BE THE STRONGEST SNOW FORT EVER BUILT!

UGHH NGGHH

RGHH MNHG UNNHH

THERE! WE'RE SAFE FROM THAT SNOW GOON *NOW*!

I WONDER WHY WE HAVEN'T SEEN HIM FOR A WHILE.

HI CALVIN. NICE SNOW FORT.

I'LL SAY! THE WALLS ARE TWO FEET THICK AND WE'VE GOT 50 SNOWBALLS IN HERE!

WHO ARE YOU FIGHTING?

THERE'S A SNOW GOON RUNNING LOOSE! IF I WERE YOU, I WOULDN'T STICK AROUND. THIS COULD GET UGLY.

WHAT'S A SNOW GOON?

IT'S LIKE A SNOW MAN, BUT A GROTESQUE, EVIL, DEMENTED MONSTER.

OH, IS *THAT* WHAT ALL THOSE UGLY THINGS YOU MADE IN THE FRONT YARD ARE?

WHAT DO YOU MEAN, "ALL THOSE"?

LOOK! A *NEW* SNOW GOON!

THAT'S NOT THE ONE I MADE!

THE ORIGINAL SNOW GOON MUST BE MAKING HIS *OWN* SNOW GOONS!

OH NO!

I'LL BET HE'S MAKING AN ARMY! IN A FEW DAYS, HE COULD BUILD A HUNDRED SNOW GOONS! IF EACH OF *THEM* BUILT *ANOTHER* HUNDRED, AND THEN *THOSE* ALL BUILT A HUNDRED *MORE*, WHY...

...THAT WOULD BE PRETTY COOL, IF THEY WEREN'T OUT TO KILL ME.

I VOTE WE MAKE TRACKS FOR FLORIDA.

89

DAD, DON'T KILL ME! I CAN EXPLAIN THIS! HELP! HELP!

SNOW GOONS! I FROZE 'EM! THEY WERE GOING TO *GET* ME, SO I HAD TO GET THEM FIRST! ASK HOBBES!

CALVIN, IT IS AFTER MIDNIGHT. BELIEVE ME, WE WILL DISCUSS THIS *VERY* THOROUGHLY TOMORROW. YOU GET INTO BED THIS INSTANT.

LIKE I'M GOING TO GET ANY SLEEP *NOW*.

SEE?? SEE THE SNOW GOONS? I DIDN'T MAKE THEM! I MEAN, I MADE *ONE*, SORT OF BY ACCIDENT, BUT THE REST MADE THEMSELVES! THEY WERE BUILDING AN ARMY, SEE?

SEE, THAT'S WHY I HAD TO FREEZE THEM LAST NIGHT! I HAD TO GET 'EM WHILE THEY WERE SLEEPING! IT WAS MY ONLY CHANCE, SEE? SEE, IT ALL MAKES SENSE!

SEE? SEE??

THEY NEVER SEE.

WELL, HOBBES, I GUESS THERE'S A MORAL TO ALL THIS.

WHAT'S THAT?

"SNOW GOONS ARE BAD NEWS."

THAT LESSON CERTAINLY OUGHT TO BE INAPPLICABLE ELSEWHERE IN LIFE.

I LIKE MAXIMS THAT DON'T ENCOURAGE BEHAVIOR MODIFICATION.

CALVIN and HOBBES

by WATTERSON

I'M HO-OME!

A TINY SNOW-MAN!

WHY ARE YOU DOWN THERE WITHOUT A COAT?

ME? NO REASON.

CALVIN and HOBBES by WATTERSON

HIS STABILIZERS USELESS, HIS FUEL ABOUT TO EXPLODE, OUR HERO CAREENS OUT OF CONTROL OVER A STRANGE, UNEXPLORED PLANET!

YES, IT'S JUST ANOTHER TYPICAL DAY FOR THE INCREDIBLE SPACEMAN SPIFF!

ZORCHED BY ZARCHES, SPACEMAN SPIFF'S CRIPPLED CRAFT CRASHES ON PLANET PLOOTARG!

DAZED BUT UNDAUNTED, OUR FEARLESS HERO SETS OFF IN SEARCH OF A SERVICE STATION!

ZOUNDS! THE ZEALOUS ZARCHES HAVE FOLLOWED SPIFF TO THE PLANET'S SURFACE TO FINISH HIM OFF!

WITH A SUDDEN CHILL, OUR HERO REALIZES THE PLANET'S SOFT, GRANULAR GROUND MAKES HIM EASY TO TRACK!

THINKING QUICKLY, SPIFF RUNS BACKWARD, SO HIS TRACKS SHOW HIM GOING THE *OPPOSITE* DIRECTION!

BY CONTINUING PAST A HIDING PLACE AND DOUBLING BACK, OUR HERO FOOLS THE HIDEOUS ALIENS!

CALVIN! IT'S TIME TO COME IN!

WE KNOW HE WENT THIS WAY. WE'LL FIND HIM.

96

TIME FOR BED, CALVIN.

YOU CAN PUT MY BODY TO BED, BUT MY SPIRIT'S GOING TO STAY RIGHT HERE, SO WHY BOTHER? WHY SHOULDN'T I JUST STAY UP?

BECAUSE THE BODY IS THE HOME OF THE SPIRIT, AND IF YOU'RE NOT IN BED IN TWO MINUTES, YOUR SPIRIT IS GOING TO BE PERMANENTLY NOMADIC.

HOME SWEET HOME.

THERE OUGHT TO BE A LAW AGAINST HAVING SCHOOL ON DAYS WHEN THERE'S ENOUGH SNOW TO PLAY IN.

OF COURSE, I DON'T THINK THERE SHOULD BE SCHOOL IN THE **FALL** EITHER ... AND SUMMER'S OUT ALREADY.... AND THEN THERE'S SPRING..

I GUESS I'D GO TO SCHOOL A DAY IN NOVEMBER AND A DAY IN MARCH.

BY SECOND GRADE, YOU'D BE PACKING YOUR LUNCH BOX WITH DENTURE CLEANERS.

AND BEFORE I GOT TO THIRD GRADE, I COULD RETIRE.

HERE COMES THE GIANT SHIP! AHWOOOOOO! AHWOOOOO!

BUT WHAT'S THIS?! HE'S GOING FULL SPEED THROUGH THE DANGEROUS STRAIT!

THE OIL TANKER CRASHED, MOM.

YOU POURED *INK* IN THE BATH WATER??

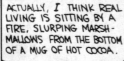

LOOK WHAT I MADE, HOBBES.

WHAT IS IT?

WHAT *IS* IT? WHY, IT'S A HUGE BIRD FOOT! I'M GOING TO PRESS IT IN THE SNOW AND MAKE EVERYONE THINK A TWO-TON CHICKADEE WALKED BY!

I GUESS TIME WEIGHS MORE HEAVILY ON SOME PEOPLE'S HANDS THAN OTHERS'.

HE'S JUST JEALOUS BECAUSE I ACCOMPLISH SO MUCH MORE THAN HE DOES.

HEY DAD, YOU KNOW HOW YOU WANTED ME TO SHOVEL THE DRIVEWAY? WELL I THOUGHT UP A *BETTER* IDEA!

I'LL SHOVEL AND PACK THE SNOW INTO A BIG RAMP! YOU CAN GET IN THE CAR, REV UP TO NEAR RED LINE, THROW OUT THE CLUTCH, LEAVE A PATCH OF MOLTEN RUBBER OUT THE GARAGE, AND ZOOM UP THE RAMP!

THEN WE COULD LINE BARRELS AND STUFF DOWN THE DRIVEWAY AND SEE HOW MANY YOU COULD CLEAR! WOULDN'T THAT BE GREAT??

I DON'T SEE WHY SOME PEOPLE EVEN *HAVE* CARS.

AUGHHH! A SNOW SNAKE'S GOT ME!

HORRIBLE INNER TEETH ON ITS SEPARATELY MOVING UPPER JAW BONES ARE PULLING ME DOWN ITS FRIGID GULLET! RUN FOR YOUR LIFE!

AT LEAST I *HAVE* A LIFE...UNLIKE SOME WEIRDOS I KNOW.

I SUPPOSE IF I HAD TWO X CHROMOSOMES, *I'D* FEEL HOSTILE TOO.

CaLVIN and HObbES

by WATTERSON

CALVIN SUDDENLY REALIZES THE WORLD HAS NO HUE, VALUE, OR CHROMA!

HAVE THE PHOTORECEPTORS IN CALVIN'S EYES STOPPED WORKING PROPERLY, OR HAS THE FUNDAMENTAL NATURE OF LIGHT CHANGED??

PERHAPS SOME STRANGE NUCLEAR OR CHEMICAL REACTION ON THE SUN HAS CAUSED ELECTROMAGNETIC RADIATION TO DEFY SEPARATION INTO A SPECTRUM!

MAYBE OBJECTS NO LONGER REFLECT CERTAIN WAVELENGTHS! WHATEVER THE CAUSE, IT'S CLEAR TO CALVIN THAT THERE'S NO POINT IN DISCUSSING THINGS WITH HIS DAD!

THE PROBLEM IS, YOU SEE EVERYTHING IN TERMS OF BLACK AND WHITE.

SOMETIMES THAT'S THE WAY THINGS ARE!!

CaLviN and HObbEs

by WATTERSON

WHILE LYING ON MY BACK TO MAKE AN ANGEL IN THE SNOW, I SAW A GREENISH CRAFT APPEAR! A GIANT UFO!

A STRANGE, UNEARTHLY HUM IT MADE! IT HOVERED OVERHEAD! AND ALIENS WERE MOVING 'ROUND IN VIEW PORTS GLOWING RED!

I TRIED TO RUN FOR COVER, BUT A HOOK THAT THEY HAD LOW'R'D SNAGGED ME BY MY OVERCOAT AND HOISTED ME ABOARD!

EVEN THEN, I TRIED TO FIGHT, AND THOUGH THEY NUMBERED MANY, I POKED THEM IN THEIR COMPOUND EYES AND PULLED ON THEIR ANTENNAE!

IT WAS NO USE! THEY DRAGGED ME TO A PLATFORM, TIED ME UP, AND WIRED TO MY CRANIUM A FIENDISH SUCTION CUP!

THEY TURNED IT ON AND CURRENT COURSED ACROSS MY CEREBELLUM, COAXING FROM MY BRAIN TISSUE THE THINGS I WOULDN'T TELL 'EM!

ALL THE MATH I EVER LEARNED, THE NUMBERS AND EQUATIONS, WERE MECHANIC'LY REMOVED IN THIS BRAIN-DRAINING OPERATION!

MY ESCAPE WAS AN ADVENTURE. (I WON'T TELL YOU WHAT I DID.) SUFFICE TO SAY, I CANNOT ADD, SO ASK SOME OTHER KID.

EARTH'S EXCESSIVE GRAVITY IS NO MATCH FOR *STUPENDOUS MAN'S* STUPENDOUS STRENGTH!

WITH MUSCLES OF MAGNITUDE, THE MASKED MAN OF MIGHT ROLLS A GIGANTIC SNOWBALL...

AND FLIES IT HIGH INTO THE STRATOSPHERE...

...WHERE HE USES HIS STUPENDOUS VISION TO LOCATE THE DIABOLICAL ARCH-FIEND *ANNOYING GIRL!*

FROM HIGH IN THE SKY, *STUPENDOUS MAN* TAKES ADVANTAGE OF EARTH'S STRONG GRAVITY!

A DIRECT HIT! *STUPENDOUS MAN* TRIUMPHS!

WITH *ANNOYING GIRL* VANQUISHED, THE WHIRLWIND WONDER ZOOMS BACK TO RESUME HIS SECRET IDENTITY!

DID YOU SAVE THE DAY?

JUSTICE REIGNS ONCE MORE!

CALVIN, SUSIE'S MOM JUST CALLED. I WANT TO TALK TO YOU.

SUSIE'S MOM SAYS YOU DROPPED A SNOWBALL THE SIZE OF A BOWLING BALL ON SUSIE FROM A TREE.

IT COULDN'T HAVE BEEN *ME!* I'M VERY MILD-MANNERED

SHE DESCRIBED EXACTLY THE HOOD AND CAPE I MADE YOU.

WHY, IT MUST'VE BEEN *STUPENDOUS MAN,* DEFENDER OF LIBERTY AND JUSTICE! I'M SURE SUSIE DESERVED WHATEVER SHE GOT.

LISTEN TO ME. YOU COULD HURT SOMEONE THAT WAY, AND IF I EVER HEAR OF ANYTHING LIKE THIS AGAIN, I'LL TAKE AWAY YOUR COSTUME FOR GOOD. GOT IT?

HMM, THIS SOUNDS LIKE *ANOTHER* JOB FOR STUPENDOUS MAN!

ACTUALLY, IT DOESN'T SOUND LIKE *QUITE* HIS TYPE OF JOB.

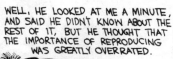

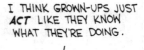

AUGH! WHO DID THIS?!

THE DAME'S SCREAM HIT AN OCTAVE USUALLY RESERVED FOR CALLING DOGS, BUT IT MEANT I HAD A CASE, AND THE SOUND OF GREENBACKS SLAPPING ACROSS MY PALM IS MUSIC TO *MY* EARS ANY DAY. AFTER ALL, I'M NOT AN OPERA CRITIC. I'M A PRIVATE EYE.

I KEEP TWO MAGNUMS IN MY DESK. ONE'S A GUN, AND I KEEP IT LOADED. THE OTHER'S A BOTTLE AND IT KEEPS *ME* LOADED. I'M TRACER BULLET. I'M A PROFESSIONAL SNOOP.

IT'S A TOUGH JOB, BUT THEN, I'M A TOUGH GUY. SOME PEOPLE DON'T LIKE AN AUDIENCE WHEN THEY WORK. ENOUGH OF THEM HAVE TOLD ME SO WITH BLUNT INSTRUMENTS THAT I'M A PHRENOLOGIST'S DREAM COME TRUE.

SNOOPING PAYS THE BILLS, THOUGH. ESPECIALLY BILL, MY BOOKIE, AND BILL, MY PROBATION OFFICER.

SO WHEN A TALL BRUNETTE OPENED MY DOOR WITH A CASE FOR ME, MY HEART DID A FEW CALISTHENICS AND I TOOK THE JOB.

THE DAME SAID SHE HAD A CASE. SHE SOUNDED LIKE A CASE HERSELF, BUT I CAN'T CHOOSE MY CLIENTS.

SHE WAS THE PUSHY TYPE. THE KIND WHO'D BREAK YOUR HEART, OR MAYBE YOUR ARMS. I HURRIED OVER.

EITHER SHE HAD A PSYCHOTIC DECORATOR, OR HER PLACE HAD BEEN RANSACKED BY SOMEONE IN A BIG HURRY.

WELL?! HOW DO YOU EXPLAIN THIS?

THE DAME WAS HYSTERICAL. DAMES USUALLY ARE.

WHAT HAVE YOU GOT TO SAY FOR YOURSELF?

DON'T TOUCH ANYTHING. I'M LOOKING FOR CLUES.

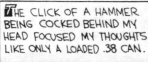

THE CLICK OF A HAMMER BEING COCKED BEHIND MY HEAD FOCUSED MY THOUGHTS LIKE ONLY A LOADED .38 CAN.

THE DAME HAD SET ME UP! SHE DIDN'T WANT ME TO SOLVE THE CASE AT ALL! SHE JUST WANTED A PATSY TO PIN THE CRIME ON!

WELL?

I DIDN'T LIKE THE WAY THIS STORY WAS SHAPING UP, SO I DECIDED TO WRITE A NEW ENDING WITH MY .45 AUTOMATIC AS CO-AUTHOR.

I INTRODUCED THE DAME TO A FRIEND WHO'S VERY CLOSE TO MY HEART. JUST A LITTLE DOWN AND LEFT, TO BE SPECIFIC.

MY FRIEND IS AN ELOQUENT SPEAKER. HE MADE THREE PROFOUND ARGUMENTS WHILE I EXCUSED MYSELF FROM THE ROOM. I ALWAYS LEAVE WHEN THE TALK GETS PHILOSOPHICAL.

YOU'RE IN *REAL* TROUBLE *NOW*, YOUNG MAN!!

I'D JUST FINISHED PUTTING THE PUZZLE PIECES TOGETHER WHEN THE DAME'S HIRED GOON JUMPED OUT OF NOWHERE AND PRACTICED FOR HIS CHIROPRACTIC DEGREE.

WHEN HE WAS DONE, AN ALL-PERCUSSION SYMPHONY WAS PLAYING IN MY HEAD, AND THE ACOUSTICS WERE INCREDIBLE. THE ORCHESTRA WENT ON A TEN-CITY TOUR OF MY BRAIN, AND I HAD A SEASON PASS WITH FRONT ROW SEATS.

I HAD FIGURED OUT WHO TRASHED THE DAME'S LIVING ROOM, BUT SINCE SHE WASN'T MY CLIENT ANY MORE, I FELT NO NEED TO DIVULGE THE INFORMATION.

BESIDES, THE CULPRIT HAPPENED TO BE A BUDDY OF MINE. I CLOSED THE CASE.

I GUESS WE SHOULD'VE PLAYED OUTSIDE, HUH?

WHAT'S UP TODAY?

NOTHING SO FAR.

"SO FAR"?

WELL, YOU NEVER KNOW. SOMETHING *COULD* HAPPEN TODAY.

AND IF ANYTHING *DOES*, BY GOLLY, I'M GOING TO BE READY FOR IT!

I NEED A SUIT LIKE THAT.

I JUST SAW A COMMERCIAL FOR A LUXURY CRUISE. HOW COME *WE* DON'T EVER GO ON VACATIONS LIKE THAT?

VACATIONS ARE ALL JUST A MATTER OF COMPARISON.

HUH?

WE SPEND A WEEK IN COLD, UNCOMFORTABLE TENTS EACH YEAR SO LIVING *HERE* THE REST OF THE TIME SEEMS LIKE A LUXURY CRUISE. IF YOUR TRIPS ARE UNPLEASANT, YOUR WHOLE *LIFE* IS A VACATION!

PLEASE TELL ME I'M ADOPTED.

YOU KNOW, I DON'T THINK MATH IS A SCIENCE. I THINK IT'S A RELIGION.

A RELIGION?

YEAH. ALL THESE EQUATIONS ARE LIKE MIRACLES. YOU TAKE TWO NUMBERS AND WHEN YOU ADD THEM, THEY MAGICALLY BECOME ONE *NEW* NUMBER! NO ONE CAN SAY HOW IT HAPPENS. YOU EITHER BELIEVE IT OR YOU DON'T.

THIS WHOLE BOOK IS FULL OF THINGS THAT HAVE TO BE ACCEPTED ON FAITH! IT'S A RELIGION!

AND IN THE PUBLIC SCHOOLS NO LESS. CALL A LAWYER.

AS A MATH ATHEIST, I SHOULD BE EXCUSED FROM THIS.

112

CALViN AND HOBBES

by WATTERSON

BOK BOK BOK
BOK

I KIND OF RESENT THE MANUFACTURER'S IMPLICIT ASSUMPTION THAT THIS WOULD AMUSE ME.

HEY DAD, HOBBES SAYS THAT TIGERS ARE MORE PERFECTLY EVOLVED THAN HUMANS!

HE SAYS THAT IF THE PLAYING FIELD WAS LEVEL AND WE DIDN'T HAVE GUNS, PEOPLE WOULD BE NOTHING BUT **CAT FOOD**! TELL HIM THAT'S NOT...

THERE! 10 CENTS.

WE BET A QUARTER, YOU CHISELER.

BU-URRPP!

CLAP
CLAP
CLAP
CLAP
CLAP
CLAP

AUTHOR! AUTHOR!

ENCORE!

PHILISTINES.

115

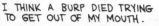

WHEN YOU'RE DONE PUTTING MY TOYS AWAY, YOU CAN GET TO WORK ON MY MATH ASSIGNMENT.

OK.

ISN'T THIS THE LIFE? WE GET TO DO WHATEVER WE WANT WHILE GOODY-TWO-SHOES HERE DOES ALL THE WORK! HE DOESN'T EVEN COMPLAIN!

VIRTUE IS ITS OWN REWARD.

HE DOESN'T COMPLAIN, BUT HIS SELF-RIGHTEOUSNESS SURE GETS ON MY NERVES.

HELLO, MAY I CARRY YOUR BOOKS FOR YOU?

WHY? SO YOU CAN THROW THEM IN A PUDDLE OR SOMETHING? FORGET IT!

I WOULDN'T DO THAT!

YEAH, YOU'D PROBABLY DO SOMETHING WORSE! YOU'RE NOT TOUCHING MY BOOKS, CALVIN!

STRICTLY SPEAKING, I'M NOT CALVIN. I'M THE PHYSICAL MANIFESTATION OF CALVIN'S GOOD SIDE.

IF THAT WAS TRUE, YOU'D BE A LOT SMALLER.

BOY, HAVE I HEARD THAT JOKE A LOT.

AND IF YOU THINK YOU CAN GET MY BOOKS BY ACTING EVEN WEIRDER THAN USUAL, THINK AGAIN!

SAY, CALVIN, THAT NICE GIRL DOWN THE STREET SEEMS TO THINK YOU'RE A TOTAL JERK.

WHO, SUSIE? YOU WEREN'T TALKING TO SUSIE, WERE YOU?

YES. I OFFERED TO CARRY HER BOOKS AND SHE...

YOU DID WHAT?!

SHE CLEARLY DOESN'T TRUST YOU AT ALL.

OH, MAN! NOBODY SAW YOU, DID THEY?! THEY'LL THINK IT WAS ME! YOU WANT TO MAKE IT LOOK LIKE I LIKE HER?!

SHE SEEMED UPSET, SO THIS AFTERNOON I TOOK HER SOME FLOWERS I PICKED, BUT...

AUGHH! AUGHH! AUGHH!

Calvin and Hobbes

by WATTERSON

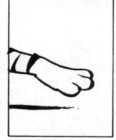

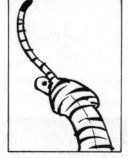

The End